MEXICAN PROVERBS

PROVERBIOS MEXICANOS

by Arturo Medina

Penfield
BOOKS

Credits

Penfield Books and Arturo Medina thank the following for their contributions:

Editor: Esther Feske

Copy Editors: Martha Perez-Bendorf, Joan Liffring-Zug Bourret, Melinda Bradnan, Miriam Canter, Deb Schense, and Whitney Pope.

Graphic Design: Esther Feske and M.A. Cook Design.

Mexican folk arts and crafts are from these collectors: Barbara Stehbens, Tom and Kathy Wegman, Stacia McGrath, Arturo Medina, and Joan Liffring-Zug Bourret.

Photos on front and back covers and page 9: Arturo Medina.

Photo page 3: Gerald Solomons, M.D.

Photos of Mayan and Mixtec sculptures are courtesy of The University of Iowa Museum of Art, the Solomons collection, with thanks to Gerald Solomons, M.D. and Dr. Hope Solomons.

All other photos of folk arts and crafts and Mexican artifacts and architecture are by Joan Liffring-Zug Bourret.

©2011 Penfield Books   Printed in U.S.A.
ISBN-13: 978-1932043693
Library of Congress Control Number: 2011927209

Chichen Itza

CONTENTS

Editor's Note

Proverbs have the advantage of being short and also the disadvantage of being short. Conciseness gives pithiness, but leaves room for many interpretations. In fact, a variety of possible meanings makes the proverb applicable in many situations, for many generations.

Some proverbs in Spanish, particularly ones that rhyme ("refranes") or that have reflexive verbs, make direct translation into English difficult. To get the translation to have the same complexity in few words is a dilemma! But in general, we have tried to give as direct a translation as possible, then Arturo's interpretation to add clarity or depth. In some cases, the Spanish proverb has a counterpart in English, so those familiar English proverbs are in quotes.

Photographs of Mexican crafts, folk art, and architecture, both ancient and contemporary, have been selected to show the visual traditions that parallel the rich oral traditions represented in this book.

We encourage our readers to "read between the lines" of these proverbs from Mexico and to find your own uses for wise old sayings. We think you will find that there are good reasons they have been passed down for generations.

—Esther Feske

DEDICATION AND ACKNOWLEDGMENTS

I dedicate this book to Susana, the bravest human being I have known in my life. As a stroke survivor she defeats adversity every day, always with a smile on her lips.

Thank you to Eliannet Acebo, Martha Covarrubias, Deyanira Isassi, Ricardo Medina, and Gloria Necoechea for their contributions. Thank you to Joan Liffring-Zug Bourret for her wonderful friendship and for conceiving the idea of this book and making it possible. Thank you to the "Ibero" for the humanistic foundation she gave me.

My deepest recognition and reverence to all of the wise people who, through many years, conceived these proverbs and to the oral tradition that kept them alive until this day as an integral part of the Mexican culture. Even though I did not get to know you in person, it is a privilege to be a recipient of your wisdom.   —Arturo Medina

Dedico este libro a Susana, el ser humano más valiente que he conocido en mi vida. Habiendo sobrevivido a un derrame cerebral ella vence a la adversidad cada día, siempre con una sonrisa en los labios.

Muchas gracias a Eliannet Acebo, Martha Covarrubias, Deyanira Isassi, Ricardo Medina, y Gloria Necoechea por sus contribuciones. Muchas gracias a Joan Liffring-Zug Bourret por su maravillosa amistad y por concebir el proyecto de este libro y hacerlo posible. Muchas gracias a la "Ibero," por la formación humanística que me diste.

Mi más profundo reconocimiento y reverencia hacia toda la gente sabia que a través de los años acuñó los proverbios, y a la tradición oral que los mantuvo vivos hasta el día de hoy como parte integral de la cultura mexicana. Aun cuando no los conocí en persona, es un privilegio ser partícipe de su sabiduría.   *—Arturo Medina*

ABOUT THE AUTHOR

Arturo and Susana Medina

"*Los dichos de los viejitos son Evangelios chiquitos.*"
Old people's sayings are tiny fragments of the Gospel.

These are personal beliefs and personal favorites.
They are ingrained in my mind and have molded
my behavior and who I am today.

I was born and raised in Mexico City, in a middle class family, my dad a chemical engineer, my mom a secretary who decided to stay home when I, her first baby, was born. I have a brother and a sister. My parents, married for 45 years now, and my brother and sister and their families, live in Mexico City.

I had the opportunity to have a privileged education and grow in a strong family with strict principles and morals. My family, like most Mexicans, is Catholic.

When time came to decide what to make out of my life, I was torn between medicine and chemical engineering. I opted for the latter, and even today I am aware I could have been a very good doctor. However, I am extremely happy with my decision and I love with passion what I do.

I got my professional chemical engineering degree from the Universidad Iberoamericana or, as we call her, "Ibero," in Mexico City. A Jesuit school, Ibero gave me the humanistic education that has been extremely important for my life.

I met my beloved wife Susana in college. We were students in the third semester, she, a nutritionist-to-be, me a chemee-to-be. It happened! It was love at first sight. At 18 years old, I knew from that very day I wanted to be with her the rest of my life. But we had to wait almost seven years before we could get married; in our culture duty comes before love, so we finished our careers and got our professional licenses, then got jobs, then a little over seventeen years ago, got married.

Our first children came right away: a beautiful set of twin girls, Sofia and Susanita. A year later we moved to the U.S. for what was supposed to be a six-month assignment, which turned out to be three years.

Shortly afterwards a job was offered to me in Iowa. We immediately fell in love with Iowa and her people. We lived there for just five years, but I feel my home in the U.S. is Iowa.

On our third year in Iowa Susana convinced me to try for another baby, and we had yet another set of twins, Victoria and Arturo, Jr. With those four wonderful children our household is full of joy and always busy; we seldom have a dull moment and we are truly blessed in them and in our wonderful friends and family.

I love to read, a habit I got from my mom, and I especially like non-technical books. I like to study Eastern philosophies and love to read classic literature, history, and psychology. I love the outdoors, cooking "asado," photography, and German shepherds.

We currently live in Austin, Texas.   —AM

Faith and Religion

A *Dios rogando y con el mazo dando.*
Praying to God and hammering away.
God is in charge of the results, I am in charge of the work and effort.

E *l hombre propone, y Dios dispone.*
Man suggests, God decides (or makes things happen).

C *omo Santo Tomas, hasta no ver, no creer.*
Like Saint Thomas, if I don't see, I don't believe.
This is said when we are skeptical of something. (Saint Thomas was the one who asked to see the resurrected Christ before believing in him.)

D *el agua mansa me libre Dios, que de la brava me guardaré yo.*
May God protect me from tranquil waters, since I'll take care of myself in turbulent waters.
We need to trust God to protect us from unforeseen dangers since we are on guard against evident ones.

D *ios aprieta pero no ahorca.*
God may squeeze you tightly, but He does not strangle you.

E *l que no habla, Dios no lo oye.*
Whoever does not speak will not be heard by God.
An admonition to pray, similar to "the squeaky wheel gets the grease."

Dios escribe derecho en renglones torcidos.
God's writing is straight, even if the lines are not.
This recognizes that the will of God always turns out right, even if we don't understand His methods.

Para sabios, Salomón.
For wise men, just Solomon.
This is used when someone asks something impossible to know. According to the Bible, only Solomon had the wisdom to know what was going to happen.

Cada mortal lleva una cruz a cuestas.
Every person has a cross to bear.

Cuando te toca, aunque te quites, y cuando no te toca, aunque te pongas.
When it is your time, it will be, even if you move out of the way; and when it is not, it will not, even if you get in the way.
This basically means that destiny will happen regardless of our will.

Nadie es profeta en su tierra.
No one is a prophet in his own land.
(This paraphrases *The Holy Bible*, Matthew 13:57.)

Dios castiga sin palo ni cuarta.
God punishes without a stick or paddle.

El diablo, harto de carne, se metió de fraile.
The devil, tired of sins of the flesh, became a friar.
Someone becomes holy only after tiring of his old ways. This could also imply that, while appearing to be a monk, he is still the devil.

El hábito no hace al monje.
The cloak does not make the monk.
"Don't judge a book by its cover."

Entre Santa y Santo, pared de cal y canto.
  Between a female saint and a male saint, better have a stone wall.

Como canta el abad, responde el sacristán.
  However the abbot sings, the sacristan will respond.

  This means that the leader shapes the behavior of the followers.

Come santo y caga Diablo.
  Takes in saint and puts out devil.

  This is used to describe hypocritical people who appear to be very upright and honest, but their actions are evil. If used as a command, it tells people to take in righteousness and eliminate evil.

Al que se ha de condenar es por demás que le recen.
  It is useless to pray for someone who is going to hell anyway.

El infierno está lleno de buenas intenciones y el cielo de buenas obras.
  Hell is full of good intentions, heaven is full of good works.

  This teaches that intentions don't count, just actions.

La caridad bien entendida empieza por uno mismo.
  Well-understood charity begins with oneself.

Cuando Dios da, hasta costales te presta.
  When God gives you something, He will even loan you the sacks to carry it.

A handmade metal candelabra holds religious candles.

No destapes un santo para tapar a otro.
Don't take the cover off one saint to put it on another.

Don't divert resources you already have allocated for one thing in order to do something else.

No es lo mismo predicar que dar trigo.
It is not the same to preach as to give wheat.

This points out the great difference between just speaking versus material fulfillment. "Actions speak louder than words."

No se acuerda el cura de cuando fue sacristán.
The priest does not remember when he was a novice.

This reminds us that the difficulties or hardships we overcome to achieve a goal are quickly forgotten.

No se puede repicar y andar en la procesión.
You cannot be tolling the bells and walk in the procession.
"You can't be in two places at the same time."

Quien quita la ocasión, quita el pecado.
Whoever eliminates the occasion, eliminates the sin.
Advises us not to create temptations.

Ladrón que roba a ladrón gana cien años de perdón.
Thief that steals from thief gains one hundred years of pardon.
It is believed that thieves are going to purgatory or hell, and that one thief stealing from another takes one hundred years off his own sentence in the afterlife.

Santo que no es visto, no es venerado.
A saint that is not seen will not be revered.
This advises that if we are not present frequently, we will be forgotten or lose favor.

Si Mahoma no va a la montaña, la montaña irá a Mahoma.
If Mohammed does not go to the mountain, the mountain will go to Mohammed.
This is used when someone goes out of his way to make something happen. I use this when I make contact with a friend I have not seen in a long time after he was supposed to get back to me.

Al que madruga, Dios le ayuda.
God helps the one who arises early.
Similar to "the early bird gets the worm."

FOOD AND DRINK

B *arriga llena, corazón contento.*
Full belly, happy heart.

Panza llena, corazón contento is another version of this saying.

A *falta de pan, tortillas.*
If there's no bread, tortillas.

Sometimes a second option is still very good.

D *el plato a la boca se cae la sopa.*
From the plate to the mouth, the soup may still fall from the spoon.

Don't think matters are accomplished until they are complete. "Almost" doesn't count.

D *e que se eche a perder a que me haga daño, mejor que me haga daño.*
If something is going to waste that hurts me, better that it hurt me.

If I have to choose between seeing food going to waste or getting sick from eating it, I'd rather get sick. Many people of my age were brought up with an acute sense of never wasting anything. The waste is considered to be worse than the hurt.

A *todo te acostumbras, menos a no comer.*
You can get used to anything, except not eating.

A *buen hambre no hay pan duro.*
There is no stale bread for the hungry.

D *e lengua me como un plato.*
I will eat a plate full of tongue.

This is a direct challenge to a blabbermouth.

A silver and ceramic tankard

Comida hecha, compañía deshecha.

Meal finished, company disperses.

This means that once a task is completed, the purpose for the group no longer exists. It can also mean that gratitude doesn't last long after the need is satisfied.

Con pan y vino se anda el camino.

With bread and wine, the road will be traveled.

This means that food and drink need to be taken care of before starting a long task.

No se pueden pedir peras al olmo.

You cannot ask for pears from the elm.

(This paraphrases a Roman maxim from the 1st century B.C.)

De la mar, el mero, y de la tierra, el carnero.
Sea bass is from the ocean, and the ram from the land.
This means that people feel comfortable in their own environments.

De limpios y tragones están llenos los panteones.
Graveyards have plenty of clean freaks and gluttons.
Both extremes can do you in. Death equalizes everyone.

Donde no hay harina, todo es mohína.
Where there is no flour, all is disgust.
A household without enough to eat will not be a happy one.

El que hambre tiene en pan piensa.
Whoever is hungry is thinking of bread.
This can refer to someone who desires something and cannot get the object of desire off his mind.

El que siembra su maíz, que se coma su pinole.
Whoever plants corn, will have *pinole* to eat.
The one who does the work will profit from it. *(Pinole* is powdered corn, sweetened.) This advises to be aware of the long-term consequences of our acts.

En la mesa y en el juego, la educación sale luego.
At the table and the card game, a person's education will be obvious.

En todos lados se cuecen habas.
Beans are cooked everywhere.
Everybody can have problems, regardless of where or who they are.

A colorful hand-painted wood platter

E *ste arroz ya se coció.*
This rice is cooked.

This means an issue is resolved.

A *lgo tendrá el agua cuando la bendicen.*
There will be something in the water when they bless it.

This suggests that there must be something bad in the water when it requires a blessing.

L *o que uno no puede ver, en su huerto le ha de nacer.*
What one cannot see will be born in his own land.

Or, whatever one cannot stand, will grow in his own garden. This implies that sometimes a strong dislike or hatred towards something actually invokes it.

Hasta lo que no come le hace daño.
Even what you don't eat can hurt you.

Even what you don't know can hurt you. This is also said of a person who is so nosy that he takes offense to everything, even if it is none of his business.

Las penas con pan son menos.
Grievances are not so bad with bread.

If we have sustenance, any other hardship will not be so bad.

Le dieron sopa de su propio chocolate.
They were given what they deserved.

This is said of a person who got a just reward or punishment for his or her actions.

Mucho ruido y pocas nueces.
Lots of noise, few pecans (nuts).

This is said of a blabbermouth who talks a lot and yields few results.

Nunca digas de esta agua no beberé.
Don't say, "I will never drink that water."

Do not judge harshly, because we may find ourselves having to do the same thing we criticize.

Una manzana podrida pudre todo el barril.
One single rotten apple will spoil the whole barrel.

This advises us to avoid bad influences, as they are contagious.

Ando como agua para chocolate.
I am like water for chocolate.

This means: I am angry. (The water used to make chocolate has to be very hot.)

Festive hand-blown glasses with multicolor spots

Un grano no hace granero, pero ayuda a su compañero.

One single grain is not a granary, but it helps.

Más vale atole con risa, que chocolate con lágrimas.

It is better to have *atole* (a humble drink) with laughter, than chocolate (a rich drink) with tears.

Aquí nomás mis chicharrones truenan.
Here only my crackers crunch.

This is said when a person is proud to have everything under control in certain circumstances. It basically means: I have it all together and under control.

No sólo de pan vive el hombre.
"Man does not live by bread alone."

VIRTUES AND VICES

Lo primero que hay que hacer para ser alguien, es parecerlo.

The first thing to do to become someone is to seem like what you want to be.

This suggests imitating the qualities and behaviors of our role models if we want to become like them.

Haz el bien y no mires a quien.

Do good unto others, and don't worry about who they are.

No hagas a otro lo que no quieres que te hagan a tí.

Don't do unto others what you don't want for yourself.

("The Golden Rule," paraphrases *The Holy Bible*, Matthew 7:12.)

Hombre prevenido vale por dos.

A man who is prepared is worth two men.

This praises a person who prevents unforeseen situations or gets ready for them beforehand; similar to the Boy Scouts motto: "Be prepared."

Más vale estar solo que mal acompañado.

It is better to be alone than in bad company.

El que por otro pide, por sí mismo aboga.

Whoever is recommending someone else is recommending himself as well.

La unión hace la fuerza.

Might comes from teamwork (working together).

The opposite is *divide y vencerás* (divide and conquer).

A folk-art angel

N *i tanto que queme al santo, ni tanto que no lo alumbre.*

Not so much (candle light) that burns the saint, or so little that doesn't light the saint.

It is customary in the Catholic tradition to burn candles for saints, represented by figures carved in wood (hence the reference to burning). This advises to get the right amount of resources to a task, not too much (to burn up the figure) or too little (leave it dark). So, the meaning is: just enough.

E *l chiste no es ser hermosa sino saber presumir.*

The point is not so much to be pretty, but to know how to present oneself.

This praises manners, elegance, and education over physical beauty.

P *rometer no empobrece, dar es lo que aniquila.*

To make promises is free, to fulfill the promises is what burdens.

Do not make promises lightly.

Agua que no has de beber, déjala correr.
Let the water run that you don't mean to drink.
Do not gather resources or possessions you don't need; let them go elsewhere.

Primero es la obligación y luego la devoción.
Obligation first, then devotion.
Devotion is something we may be fond of, and is admirable, but it is not required from us. This teaches us to take care of our mandatory duties first, then spend time or resources on the secondary activities, even if we are fond of them.

A camino largo, paso corto.
Short stride for a long journey.
Means both "every long journey starts with a single step" and "pace yourself."

El que va lento, llega lejos.
Whoever walks slowly will walk far.

Más vale maña que fuerza.
Skill is better than strength.

El buen juez por su casa empieza.
A good judge begins justice in his own household.
We cannot pretend to preach or perform what we don't practice ourselves.

La conquista de uno mismo es la mayor de las victorias.
Self mastering is the greatest of victories.

Si al hablar no has de halagar, lo mejor es callar.
If while speaking you have nothing good to say, it is best to be quiet.

La verdad no peca, pero incomoda.
Truth does not sin, but it is inconvenient.
Telling the truth is not sinful, but confronting the truth makes people uncomfortable.

En boca cerrada no entran moscas.
A closed mouth gathers no flies.

El que la sigue la consigue.
Whoever follows it, will get it.
Be persistent in the pursuit of our goals.

Haz buenas acciones y recibirás bendiciones.
Do good deeds and you will be blessed.

La virtud a fuerza, no es virtud.
Virtue that needs to be enforced is not truly a virtue.
Virtue must be voluntary to be considered as such.

No te preocupes, mejor ocúpate.
Don't worry; better get busy.

Obras son amores, y no buenas razones.
Good deeds are based on acts, not good excuses.

La palabra es plata y el silencio es oro.
Word is silver, silence is gold.

No hay fecha que no llegue, ni plazo que no se cumpla.
Every date will arrive, and every period of time will expire.
This reminds us that time passes and to get things started, even things that will take a long time.

El que nada debe, nada teme.
Whoever owes nothing, fears nothing.
Whoever has a clean conscience is fearless.

Quien mucho se baja, el culo enseña.
Whoever gets too low (as in bowing), will expose his bottom.
Avoid excessive humility lest we humiliate ourselves.

Más vale sentirse defraudado que defraudar al que lo necesita.
It is better to feel let down than to let down someone in need.

El hombre no ha de ser de dichos sino de hechos.
A man must not be of sayings, but of doings.

Más vale una colorada que cien descoloridas.
It is better to be red-faced than a hundred times colorless.
Be clear immediately, even if embarrassed, rather than being wimpy or "beating around the bush".

No hay peor ciego que el que no quiere ver.
There is no one more blind than he who does not want to see.
This is said in frustration when someone refuses to face the facts or listen to advice.

No hay peor sordo que el que no quiere oír.
There is no one more deaf than the one who does not want to listen.

El que no oye consejo, no llega a viejo.
Whoever does not listen to advice will not make it to old age.

A demon with many heads and a forked tongue

Quien mal empieza, mal acaba.
Whoever starts badly will end up badly.

De desagradecidos está el infierno lleno.
Hell is full of ungrateful people.

Pueblo chico, infierno grande.
Small town, big hell.

This is said about gossip and hearsay in small towns.

Ganar uno y gastar dos no tiene perdón de Dios.
Earn one and spend two has no forgiveness from God.

This teaches never to spend more than we make.

Lo mejor de los dados es no jugarlos.
The best thing one can do with dice is not to roll them.

25

Afortunado en el juego, desafortunado en amores.
Fortunate in gambling, unfortunate in love.

There is a belief that love and luck in gambling are incompatible.

El que no mira hacia adelante, atrás se queda.
(Quien adelante no mira, atrás se queda.)
Whoever doesn't look forward falls behind.

Entre más grandotes, más pesados caen.
The bigger they are, the harder they fall.

Aquel que anda por la sierra cualquier día se desbarranca.
He who walks in the mountains may some day fall from the heights.

No juzgues a nadie antes de haber caminado un kilómetro en sus zapatos.
Don't make any judgments about anyone until you have walked one mile in their shoes.

No hay que hacer caravana con sombrero ajeno.
Do not try to obtain something wearing another's hat.

Do not claim credentials you do not have; you may have to prove it.

Aprendiz de todo y maestro de nada.
Apprentice of everything and master of nothing.

Warns against trying to learn too many things without becoming expert of anything.

Mal de muchos, consuelo de tontos.
Ailment of many, fool's consolation.

This advises against justifying one's vices just because "everybody does it."

Ancient Mexican "Wind God"

Quien siembra vientos recoge tempestades.
Whoever plants winds harvests hurricanes.

Al que al cielo escupe, en la cara le cae.
Whoever spits to the sky gets it back on his face.

En la boca del mentiroso lo cierto se hace dudoso.
In the mouth of a liar even the truth is dubious.

Una mentira mil veces repetida, adquiere la categoría de verdad.
A lie repeated a thousand times acquires the rank of truth.

El que mete mano en bolsa ajena, se condena.
He who puts his hand into someone else's purse condemns himself.

La avaricia rompe el saco.
Greediness breaks the sack.

By being greedy, one risks losing everything.

LESSONS FROM THE ANIMALS

Más vale pájaro en mano que ver un ciento volando.

It is better to have one bird in the hand than seeing one hundred in flight.

This praises accomplishments and results rather than prospects of success.

A caballo regalado, no le mires el diente.

Don't look into a gift horse's mouth.

Don't criticize something that is given to us for free.

A otro perro con ese hueso.

Go to another dog with that bone.

This means: I already know that trick. This is used when someone tries to persuade us to do something we already know not to do, or when someone tries to trick us, and we do not fall into the trap.

Al ojo del amo engorda el caballo.

The horse grows strong under the owner's direct supervision.

This teaches us to directly supervise our own affairs if we want them to go well.

De que la mula dice "No paso" y la mujer "Me caso" la mula no pasa y la mujer se casa.

If a mule says "I will not walk" and a woman "I will marry," the mule will not walk, and the woman will marry.

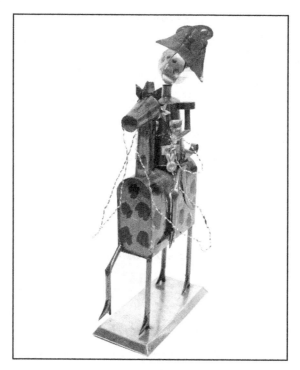

Tin man on horseback

El que por su gusto es buey, hasta la coyunta lame.
Whoever is content to be an ox will even kiss his yoke.

When someone is content with a situation, he will embrace the discomforts of such condition.

Muerto el perro, se acabó la rabia.
Once the dog is dead, the rabies are ended.

This is said about a drastic remedy for some situations. It also could mean that when you have dealt with the source of the problem, the problem is gone.

Se puede llevar un caballo al agua, pero no obligarlo a beber.
"You can lead a horse to water, but you can't make him drink."

Camarón que se duerme se lo lleva la corriente.
A shrimp that falls asleep is carried away by the current.

This praises constant vigilance so we don't get carried away by life's tides.

El buey suelto bien se lame.
A free ox knows how to care for himself.

People know how to take care of themselves if we let them.

Según el sapo, es la pedrada.
Depending on the size of the toad will be the size of the rock.

Match your resources and tools to the task at hand.

Una golondrina no hace verano.
A single swallow doesn't make the summer.

An early indication of something does not mean that the main event is here.

Al que mata un perro, le dicen mataperros.
Whoever kills a dog is called dog killer.

You will be known for what you do.

Gallo que no canta, algo tiene en la garganta.
A rooster that does not crow has something in its throat.

If someone doesn't do something, maybe it's because they can't.

No se hizo la miel para la boca del asno.
Honey was not intended to be eaten by donkeys.

Similar to "Don't cast pearls before swine," from *The Holy Bible*, Matthew 7:6.

Folk-art painted wood rabbit

Donde menos se piensa, salta la liebre.
The hare will jump out from the least expected place.

A reminder to look in unexpected places for a problem or a solution.

El pez por su boca muere.
The fish dies due to its mouth.

Keep your mouth closed if you don't want to get caught.

El pez grande se come al pequeño.
The large fish eats the small one.

Hazte miel, y te comerán las moscas.
Turn yourself into honey and you will be eaten by flies.

If we are too kind or too sweet, we risk being taken advantage of.

La cabra siempre tira al monte.
The goat always goes to the mountain.
This recognizes the nature of people to return to their origins.

Las águilas andan solas, los borregos en manada.
Eagles fly alone; sheep stay in herds.

Más vale ser cabeza de ratón que cola de león.
It is better to be the head of a mouse than the tail of a lion.
This advocates leadership, even on a small scale, rather than following the crowd.

Se quedó como el perro de las dos tortas.
He/she was left with the dog of the two bones.
This is a reference to the fable of a dog that has a bone in his mouth, goes to drink from a pool, and sees his reflection in the water. He loses his own bone when he tries to steal the bone from the dog in the reflection. This advises: don't be too greedy, don't confuse fiction with reality, and don't give up something we already possess for what we covet.

Me extraña que siendo araña te caigas de la pared.
It surprises me that, being a spider, you have just fallen off the wall.
This is said to a person who makes a mistake at something they are usually very good at.

Arrancón de caballo brioso y sentón de burro penco.
Starts like a thoroughbred and falls back like an old donkey.
Said about a fast-paced start followed by a dramatic slowdown.

Multicolored folk-art hummingbird

Pájaro viejo no entra en jaula.
An old bird will not enter a cage.

Puro pájaro nalgón.
Just a bird with a big butt.
Since a fat bird can't fly, this is derogatory and is
said of someone who fails to prove with action or
results what had been promised.

Quien bien quiere a Beltrán, bien quiere a su can.
Whoever loves Beltran will love his dog too.
This means that liking a master and his dog go
together. (Beltran is a generic name.)

Aún no ensillamos y ya cabalgamos.
**We have not saddled yet and we're galloping
already.**
"We're getting ahead of ourselves" or "we don't have
all the bases covered yet."

Aramos, le dijo la mosca al buey.
"We're plowing," said the fly to the ox.
This is used when a bystander tries to get credit for
something another person is doing.

MONEY

Con dinero baila el perro.
With money, the dog will dance.

The task at hand will be done once the payment is
made. Or, with enough money, you can get someone
to do what they could not normally do.

Contra el vicio de pedir hay la virtud de no dar.
**Against the vice of borrowing money, there exists
the virtue of not lending it.**

In dealing with people who are in the habit of asking
for money or goods, this recommends not lending,
but letting them earn for themselves.

Cuando el dinero no entra por la puerta, el amor se
va por la ventana.
**When money doesn't come in through the door,
love will leave through the window.**

De poquito en poquito, se llena el jarrito.
Little by little, the jar fills up.

Constant savings will eventually fill the piggy bank.

El que todo lo ajeno quiere, todo lo suyo pierde.
**Whoever desires all that does not belong to them
will lose all of their own possessions.**

Al buen pagador no le duelen prendas.
A good payer gets to keep his possessions.

Dando y dando, pajarito volando.
Give and take as quickly as a bird flies.

We must pay for something at the same time that we
receive it.

"El Rey", a king mask

Poderoso caballero es Don Dinero.
Mr. Money is a powerful gentleman indeed.
(This is often quoted from a poem by Francisco de Quevedo, famous Spanish writer.)

Hijo de rico: caballero, nieto limosnero.
Son of a rich man, a knight; grandson of the same, beggar.
This reflects the belief that the skill to make money can be passed down one generation but not two, or that children who grow up rich do not necessarily make or increase fortunes.

Tanto tienes, tanto vales.
So much you have, so much you're worth.
One way to measure a person's worth is to measure what they own.

El dinero es de papel para que vuele y de moneda para que ruede.

Money is made of paper so it can fly, and a coin is round so it can roll.

"Easy come, easy go."

Dinero llama dinero.

Money calls money.

Money attracts more money.

El que parte y reparte, se queda con la mejor parte.

Whoever splits and shares, keeps the better part for himself.

El que quiera azul celeste, que le cueste.

Whoever desires sky-blue color will have to pay the price.

This advises us to pay the price of what we wish for. (In this context *azul celeste* means beautiful and desirable, or the ideal of what we seek.)

El que tuvo, retuvo, y guardó para la vejez.

Whoever had, held, and saved for old age.

No vendas la piel del oso antes de haberlo matado.

Don't sell the bear's hide before killing it.

"Don't count your chickens before they're hatched."

No todo lo que reluce es oro.

Not all that shines is gold.

ON ADVERSITY

A *mal tiempo, buena cara.*
To bad times, a good face, or put a good face to bad weather.

Develop a good attitude in the face of adversity.

A *l mal paso darle prisa.*
Go through bad or bitter situations quickly.

Don't dwell on a bad experience; move on.

L *o que no mata, engorda.*
What doesn't kill you, fattens.

Adversity that doesn't kill you makes you stronger.

C *ada quien sabe dónde le aprieta el zapato.*
Everyone knows where his own shoe rubs.

No one but the subject can say exactly where their discomfort is. Also implied is: each person knows best where they can make improvements.

C *ada quien es dueño de su miedo.*
Each person is owner of their own fear.

E *l león no es tan fiero como lo pintan.*
The lion is not as fierce as he is painted.

This teaches us not to exaggerate our fear of someone or something based on hearsay.

I *r por lana y volver trasquilado.*
Going for wool and returning sheared.

This refers to a misfortune: going to obtain something (wool from sheep, or money) and returning the loser, for whatever reason. In English, it's called "getting fleeced."

Mayan ceramic pot with skulls

Con paciencia y reflexión se aprovecha la ocasión.
With patience and contemplation one can make the most of any occasion.

This comes from one of my favorite books "Astucia" by Luis G. Inclan.

Cuando está más oscuro, es que está a punto de amanecer.
The darkest part of the night is just before dawn.

Después de la tempestad viene la calma.
After the tempest comes calm.

La desgracia pone a prueba a los amigos y descubre a los enemigos.
Disgrace tests friends and uncovers enemies.

When trouble strikes, you discover who your real friends and enemies are.

El que persevera, alcanza.
Who perserveres, achieves.

No hay mal que por bien no venga.
There is no bad from which good does not come.

Quien canta, sus males espanta.
Whoever sings makes his grievances go away.

Quien bien te quiere te hará llorar.
Whoever loves you will make you cry.

Echando a perder se aprende.
Learning happens by making mistakes.

No hay peor lucha que la que no se hace.
There is no worse attempt than the one that is never made.
Do not feel defeated before you even start.

A rey muerto, rey puesto.
Another king will replace the one that just died.
Life goes on, even if the current situation seems catastrophic.

Pobreza no es vileza.
Poverty is not contemptible.
This means that just because someone is poor does not mean that they are mean or depraved.

La necesidad tiene cara de hereje.
Necessity has the face of a heretic.
If a person needs something he may not follow the rules to get it done. Also, hardship pays no attention to appearances; someone going through hard times will not be choosy or picky.

"Bound Captive," a Mayan ceramic sculpture

E *n este mundo traidor nada es verdad ni mentira,
todo es del color del cristal con que se mira.*
**In this treacherous world, nothing is true or
false; it all depends of the color of the glass one
is looking through.**

D *ías de mucho, vísperas de nada.*
Today I have much, yesterday nothing.
This encourages us that many times abundance will
follow a period of loss, or rain will follow drought.

N *adie sabe lo que tiene, hasta que lo pierde.*
No one knows what he has until he loses it.

D *esnudo nací, desnudo me hallo: ni pierdo ni gano.*
I was born naked, I am naked: I'm breaking even.
This warns of the futility of accumulating goods in
this world, as we came into it naked and will leave
naked, too.

Relationships and Family

El hombre ha de tener una vieja y una mula, pero que la vieja no sea mula y que la mula no sea vieja.

A man should have a wife and a mule, but the old lady should not be stubborn and the mule should not be old.

This is word-play in Spanish, where *mula* means both mule and stubborn, and *vieja* means wife and old.

A la mujer ni todo el amor, ni todo el dinero.

To a woman, (give) neither all your love nor all your money.

El caballo, la pistola y la mujer, no los prestes a nadie.

The horse, the gun, and the woman, never loan to anyone.

A una mujer no se la debe tocar ni con el pétalo de una rosa.

A woman must not be touched (hit) even with the petal of a rose.

This is a warning against disrespectful behavior.

Hay que quererlas, no hay que entenderlas.

You have to love them; you don't have to understand them.

This could apply when a man is trying to figure out how women's minds work and how to make them happy: don't try to understand those intricacies, just love them the way they are.

Amor con amor se paga.
Love has to be paid with love.

Consider that money may not be a valid currency for many of life's most important trades.

Antes que te cases, mira lo que haces.
Take a close look at what you're doing before getting married.

A las mujeres y a los charcos no hay que andarles con rodeos.
For women and ponds, you better not beat around the bush.

This advises a direct, straightforward approach when dealing with women.

Al cabo cuando ellas quieren, solitas se dan lugar.
At the end, when they so decide, they get their position by themselves.

This recognizes that women choose whom they want to be with, and when they do, they make it happen.

Carta que se niega y mujer que se va, no hay que irlas a buscar.
A request that has been denied and a woman who has gone, there is no need to search further.

Cuando una mujer avanza, no hay hombre que retroceda.
When a woman steps forward, no man will retreat.

Detrás de un gran hombre siempre hay una gran mujer.
Behind a great man is always a great woman.

Great men always accomplish such feats thanks to the support of great women in their lives.

Mayan "Corn Maiden" lies on a metate *(corn-grinding stone)*

Con la que entiende de atole y metate con esa cásate.

> **Marry the one who is a good cook (who understands *atole* and *metate*).**
>
> *Atole* is a corn-based drink. A *metate* is the stone on which one grinds corn into flour.

Donde hubo fuego, cenizas quedan.

> **Where there was fire, hot ashes and embers remain.**
>
> This talks about both the nature of fire and the nature of love. Both can easily reignite.

Es más fácil contener la corriente de un rio que a la mujer cuando se obstina.

> **It is easier to contain the waters of a river than a woman who has decided to get something done.**

Gallina vieja hace buen caldo.

> **An old hen makes good soup.**
>
> This praises the qualities of older women.

Dios los cría y ellos se juntan.
God made them, and they found each other.
This is often said of couples that are very much like each other or get along very well.

La mujer compuesta quita el marido de otra puerta.
The confident woman takes the husband from another door.
A warning that a woman who thinks she can will likely steal another's husband.

La que de amarillo se viste, en su hermosura confía, o de sinvergüenza se pasa.
She who dresses in yellow is confident of her beauty or is shameless.
In the past, wearing yellow had negative or risqué connotations.

La mujer es fuego, el hombre estopa, viene el diablo y sopla.
The woman is fire, the man, tinder, and the devil comes and blows.

La mujer es como el vidrio, siempre está en peligro.
A woman is like glass: always at risk.
Take good care of a woman or you may lose her, just as glass, once broken, cannot be fixed.

Mujer a quien le das lo que te pide, mujer que te dará lo que le pidas.
A woman to whom you give what she asks is a woman who will give you what you ask.

No hay mujeres imposibles, sólo hombres incapaces.
There are no impossible women, just incapable men.

Mujer y sardina para sabrosa, chiquitina.
Women and sardines are more pleasurable when small.

No hay bonita sin pero, ni fea sin gracia.
There is no pretty woman without imperfection, nor an ugly one without attributes.

No hay quince años feos ni viuda rica despreciable.
There is no ugly debutante nor despicable rich widow.

Ni buscarlas si se han ido, ni echarlas si no se van.
Don't search for women if they leave nor throw them out if they stay.

Se quedó como novia de rancho, vestida y alborotada.
She was left like a poor bride, all dressed up and restless.
This is said when someone is expecting something to happen and it does not, like a bride ready for the ceremony and the groom does not show up.

Toda mujer tiene sus cinco minutos.
Every woman has her five minutes.
This is said of a woman's beauty, fame, power, anger, upset, craziness, etc.

Una mujer despechada es peor que un león marihuano.
An upset, angry woman is more dangerous than a crazed lion.

Para gato viejo, ratón tierno.
For the old cat, a young, tender mouse.
This refers to an attraction older men feel towards younger women.

Casamiento y mortaja, del cielo baja.
Marriage and funeral shroud come down from Heaven.
It is advice not to worry about who we are going to marry or when we are going to die, as we should leave those matters to God. This may seem fatalistic, which is very Mexican.

En la guerra y en el amor todo es permitido.
In warfare and in love everything is permitted.
"All's fair in love and war."

Lo que no fue en tu año, no fue en tu daño.
What did not happen in your time did not damage you.
This could be said to someone who feels jealous of former relationships of their partner.

Los hijos y los maridos por sus hechos son queridos.
Children and husbands for their deeds are loved.

Marido que no da, y cuchillo que no corta, si se pierde, nada importa.
The husband that does not provide and the knife which does not cut are not missed if they get lost.

No niega la cruz de su parroquia.
He does not deny the cross of his own parish.
I use this saying when I notice resemblance in families, like a grandson or granddaughter looking like their grandparent. Another interpretation is: he does not disparage where he came from.

Reloj, caballo y mujer, tener bueno o no tener.
Watch, horse, and woman; better have good ones or none at all.

An airy covered portal *(porch)*

U*n clavo saca a otro clavo.*
A nail gets another one out.

The new drives out the old. This is often used about relationships: a new girlfriend or boyfriend will get us over an earlier one.

U*n viejo amor ni se olvida ni se deja.*
An old love is neither forgotten nor left behind.

E*l que mucho se despide, pocas ganas tiene de irse.*
Whoever lingers in goodbyes is not really willing to leave.

De tal palo, tal astilla.
Like stick, like splinter.
"Like father, like son."

Hijo de tigre, pintito.
Son of a tiger, has stripes.
"Like father, like son."

Un hermano no siempre es un amigo, pero un amigo es siempre un hermano.
A brother is not always a friend, but a friend is always a brother.

A quien Dios no le dio hijos, el diablo le dio sobrinos.
To whom God did not give children, the devil gave nephews and nieces.

Cría a tus hijos con un poco de hambre y un poco de frío.
Raise your children with a little hunger and a little cold.
This advises us to not give our children all they want.

Los niños y los borrachos siempre dicen la verdad.
Children and drunks always tell the truth.

Madre que a su hijo consiente, va engordando una serpiente.
A mother who spoils her child is feeding a poisonous snake.

A la vejez, viruelas.
Chicken pox to an elder.
This is said when an older person commits mistakes normally associated with youth.

Beautiful arches frame the view of a Mexican hotel courtyard.

Cuando joven, de ilusiones, cuando viejo, de recuerdos.

When young, illusions; when old, memories.

A reminder of the source of speaking and actions.

Cuando tu vas, yo ya vengo.

When you go, I'm already returning.

This reminds younger people that the experience of elders is very valuable, and it is likely that they have gone through the situation we are facing. Deep reverence for our elders is a cornerstone of Mexican culture.

El que espera, desespera.

Whoever hopes and waits will despair.

Simply hoping and waiting do not improve the situation, and disappointment is likely.

Al que se aleja lo olvidan, y al que se muere lo entierran.

He who leaves is forgotten, and he who dies is buried.

Similar to "out of sight, out of mind" in English.

Amigo reconciliado, enemigo doblado.

Reconciled friend, hidden enemy.

This warns that once a friendship is restored after a serious problem, it will never be the same, or it may even be dangerous, and that "friend" could always be a threat.

Amarra navajas.

Sheathe knives.

A command to be careful of things with dangerous potential. This is said of a person who incites fights.

Cría cuervos y te sacarán los ojos.

Breed ravens, and they will take out your eyes.

If you create problems that seem innocuous when small, they can grow into big problems. Similar to: "If you play with fire, you will get burned."

Criados, enemigos pagados.

Servants: paid enemies.

This saying questions the loyalty and trustworthiness of permanent servants in the household, as they have access to intimate knowledge of the household and have often helped robbers by tipping them off or allowing access to the house.

Chula a quien mucho se chulea, se le obliga a que lo crea.

A cute girl whom everyone says is cute, ends up believing it.

You become what everyone tells you that you are.

A vine-covered ramada in an architect's home.

Al que ven caballo, le ofrecen silla.
To him who is seen as a horse, they offer a saddle.
People will treat you to match how you act.

El que es perico dondequiera es verde, y el que es pendejo, dondequiera pierde.
He who is a parrot is green everywhere, and he who is stupid loses everywhere.

Cada loco con su tema.
Each crazy with his own theme.
This refers to conversations where there is a lack of communication, or situations where people truly don't understand each other, or truly disagree.

Cada quien se pone la corona que labra.
Everyone wears the crown of their own making.
Everyone has the life they created.

Cada quien se rasca con sus uñas.
Everyone scratches himself with his own nails.
"Every man for himself."

Cada quien tiene su forma de matar las pulgas.
Everyone has their own way of killing fleas.
"There are a thousand ways to skin a cat."

Están más cerca los dientes que los parientes.
Your own teeth are closer (to yourself) than your relatives.
This advises you to feed yourself first, then share your food with relatives. Or fend for yourself first, since no one can give what he or she does not have.

Del árbol caído todos hacen leña.
Once a tree is fallen, everyone will make firewood.
A warning that when someone's position of advantage or prestige is lost, others will take advantage of them.

Al que no le saben, le inventan.
That which is not known is invented.
Stories will be invented in the absence of facts.

En esta vida todo se sabe, y lo que no, se hace chisme.
In this life everything is eventually known, and what is not, becomes gossip.

Al son que le toquen, baila.
Dance to the tune they play.
Behave appropriate to the circumstances.

El muerto y el arrimado a los tres días apestan.
The corpse and the visitor stink after three days.

An *arrimado* is a person who moves into a household due to an emergency, normally uninvited. This saying advises that we limit our stay with friends or family, even in emergencies, to no more than three days.

Ni pidas a quien pidió, ni sirvas a quien sirvió.
Don't ask money from a former beggar, nor serve a former servant.

People who have suffered and overcome hardships frequently have no sympathy for other people going through the same experiences.

El que no vive para servir, no sirve para vivir.
Whoever does not live for helping others is not making good use of their life.

This teaches us that being of service is a cornerstone of a good life.

Caras vemos, corazones no conocemos.
We can see faces, but cannot see hearts.

While we can see physical appearance, true feelings are not seen with the eyes. It can also be a warning that although someone looks pleasant and good-natured, you cannot really tell what that person's intentions are.

El que de tu casa se aleja, de la suya te retira.
Whoever distances himself from your household (or friendship) is also distancing you from his.

In Mexico it is customary that close friendships happen at home. If we open our home to someone, it is a sign of close friendship and trust. This advises that if someone is distancing himself from us, that means the friendship has cooled, and we should respect that.

Le dan la mano y se toma hasta el brazo.
He is given a hand and takes the whole arm.
This is said of abusive people who take advantage of help offered to them. "Give him an inch and he'll take a mile."

Entre sastres no se cobran hechuras.
Among tailors they don't charge each other for alterations.
This refers to friends or colleagues that help each other for free.

La ropa sucia se lava en casa.
Dirty laundry gets washed at home.
Take care of uncomfortable family affairs in private. "Don't air your dirty laundry in public."

No hay que mentar la soga en casa del ahorcado.
Don't mention the hangman's noose in the house of someone who was hanged.
This advises us of being sensitive to family situations and avoid sore or painful subjects when we are with family members.

Ninguno diga quién es, sus obras lo dirán.
No one needs to say who he is, his works will say it.

Calladita te ves más bonita.
You look prettier when you stay quiet.
This praises silence. "God gave us two ears and just one mouth—to listen more than we talk."

El que calla, otorga.
Whoever remains silent, consents.
Silence gives consent.

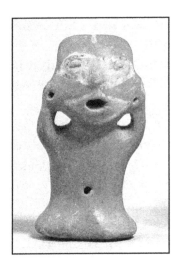

"The Scream," a small Mayan pottery sculpture

L *as personas silenciosas siempre son peligrosas.*
Silent (quiet, reserved) people always are dangerous.

This caution is contradicted by other proverbs which advocate being quiet!

On the other hand, this proverb suggests that being quiet, concentrating on what you're doing, can make you "dangerous." This is not necessarily a bad thing, since here I interpret it as "competent."

M *as rápido cae un hablador que un cojo.*
A blabbermouth falls sooner than the lame.

L *a sonrisa que no viene del corazón se llama hipocresía.*
The smile that does not come from the heart is called hypocrisy.

L *a suerte de la fea, la bonita la desea.*
The luck of the ugly is desired by the beautiful.

There is a common belief that good-looking women are not as lucky as average-looking or ugly ones.

No hay bien ni mal que cien años dure, ni tarugo que los aguante.

There is no good or bad which lasts one hundred years, nor a fool who puts up with either.

No es santo de mi devoción.

That is not a saint I am devoted to.

This is said of a person the speaker is not fond of, similar to "he or she is not my cup of tea."

No tiene vela en el entierro.

He has no candle in the burial.

This is said of a person who has no business being involved in a given situation.

Ni picha, ni cacha, ni deja batear.

Doesn't pitch, doesn't catch, and doesn't let anyone be at bat.

This is said of a person who wants to be in the middle of everything and does nothing.

La manzana podrida pierde su compañía.

The rotten apple loses its companionship.

A person who turns for the worse is left alone.

Quien a buen árbol se arrima, buena sombra le cobija.

Whoever gets under a good tree enjoys good shade.

Choose good friends and acquaintances so you can enjoy their influence.

Arajarse a su tierra.

If you are going to give up, go home.

I use this saying as a challenge to hold on tight, and don't give up. It has tremendous meaning for us immigrants.

SUCCESS AND BUSINESS

Cada quien tiene la suerte que se granjea.
Everyone has the luck he/she builds.
Similar to a couple of wise sayings in English: "Go out and make your own luck," and "Seems like the harder I work, the more luck I have."

Es mejor pedir perdón que pedir permiso.
It is better to ask forgiveness than permission.
This praises boldness and initiative in doing what you need to do; if you are wrong, then ask forgiveness.

El mundo es de los audaces.
The world belongs to the audacious.

A río revuelto, ganancia de pescadores.
Murky river means fishermen's gain.
Often times confusion means huge profits for opportunistic people.

El que tiene padrino, se bautiza.
Whoever has a godfather will get baptized.
A person who has the resources to accomplish something will get it done.

El que da obliga, y el que recibe, queda obligado.
Whoever gives something to someone makes that person feel obliged to reciprocate, and whoever receives something is likewise obliged.
One of the oldest rules of human communities: reciprocity.

No gastes tu pólvora en infiernitos.
Don't waste your powder making little fires.

Don't waste your resources in small approaches for a task. It is better to save them to accomplish the big task at hand.

Dime de qué presumes, y te diré de qué careces.
Tell me what you show off, and I'll tell you what you are lacking.

A grandes males, grandes remedios.
Big ailments, big remedies.

Sometimes there are situations that require drastic, definitive action.

El que da y quita con el diablo se desquita.
Whoever gives and takes (away) will get even with the devil.

This condemns giving something and then taking back; you will eventually have to get even with the evil one. Or, if you try to take advantage, you will owe the Devil.

El que tenga tienda, que la atienda, y si no, que la venda.
He who has a store, let him take care of it, and if not, let him sell it.

No prestes dinero a un amigo, pierdes el dinero, y pierdes al amigo.
Don't lend money to a friend, since you will lose your money and your friend.

I also honor the other side of this proverb: never borrow money from a friend. In my scale of values, friendship is more valuable, and I wouldn't like to lose a friend if, for whatever reason, I can't pay him back.

Multi-colored hand-painted pottery is popular with Mexicans and tourists alike.

No cuentes dinero enfrente de los pobres.
Do not count money in front of the poor.

La ocasión hace al ladrón.
The opportunity makes the thief.

Quien todo lo quiere, todo lo pierde.
Whoever wants everything will lose everything.

This tells us to limit ourselves; don't be too ambitious.

Lo prometido es deuda.
A promise becomes a debt.

This teaches us to fulfill our promises and therefore not to promise lightly.

Lo barato sale caro.
Cheap stuff is expensive.

This warns us against buying cheap things or services based on price only; their poor quality will cause us to buy the same things several times over.

Salió mas caro el caldo que las albóndigas.
The soup turned out to be more expensive than the meatballs.

This is said when the add-ons to something increase the original price tremendously.

Por la muestra se conoce el paño.
You can tell the quality of a cloth from a little sample of it.

De los cuarenta para arriba no te mojes la barriga.
After forty, don't get your tummy wet.

This warns to not do very stressful or risky work after forty years of age.

De noche todos los gatos son pardos.
At night, all cats are black.

There are situations where a difference cannot be seen among similar issues.

No es lo mismo Chana que Juana.
Chana is not the same as Juana.

This is used when comparing two situations which may appear equivalent, but turn out to be completely different.

Más vale tarde que nunca.
Better late than never.

For a commitment or an appointment, it is better to show up or fulfill it late than not at all. (This saying was recorded as early as the first century B.C.)

A fanciful folk-art bear holds a fish in its mouth.

No se puede obtener un bebe en un mes con nueve mujeres embarazadas.

You cannot get a baby in one month with nine pregnant women.

Some processes just take their time, and are not a matter of throwing more resources at an issue, but understanding the nature of time. This is useful in project management.

Roma no se hizo en un día.

Rome was not built in one day.

Large projects take a long time to be accomplished. (This proverb was first published in 1546.)

No hay que empezar la casa por el tejado.

When building the house, don't start with the roof.

No cuentes tus pollos antes de nacer.

Don't count your chickens before they hatch.

Vísteme despacio, que llevo prisa.
Dress me slowly; I'm in a hurry.

This, I was told, was what Napoleon used to say to his chamber assistant. It means that when we are in a hurry to get something done, we need to slow down and take care to do it right the first time, since we don't have time for corrections. (Augustus Caesar — 63 B.C.–A.D. 14 — said "More haste, less speed.")

No se puede chiflar y comer pinole.
You cannot whistle and eat *pinole* at the same time.

Pinole is a sweet, powdered corn which is very dry, and so eating it dries the saliva in the mouth, making it impossible to whistle. The meaning is that two tasks that are fundamentally different cannot be performed at the same time.

No da paso sin huarache.
They don't take a step without sandals.

This is said of a person who knows exactly what he/she is doing, and has taken all things into consideration before engaging in a task. It is used as praise for someone who is very competent.

A ver de qué cuero salen más correas.
Let's see which leather will yield more straps.

This is a challenge to match your results to mine.

No da pie con bola.
Cannot get his foot to kick the ball.

This is said of a person who has no clue on what he or she is doing.

El que a dos amos sirve, con alguno queda mal.
Whoever serves two masters will eventually fail one of them.

An amusing lavendar and turquoise anteater

D *onde manda capitán, no gobierna marinero.*
Where there is a captain in charge of a vessel, the sailor has no authority.

This is said to recognize authority, such as: "You're in charge here," or "I am not the authority here."

L *as escaleras se barren de arriba para abajo.*
Stairs must be cleaned from the top down.

The political and entrepreneurial correlations of this saying are obvious.

M *ariachi pagado toca mal son.*
A musician paid in advance will not perform well.

C *ayendo el muerto y soltando el llanto.*
I'll start crying as soon as the dead man drops.

This means that the task will not be started (or paid) until all of the requirements are met. Do your part, then I'll do mine.

Casa con dos puertas, mala es de guardar.
 A house with two doors is a problem to keep safe.

De fuera vendrá quien de casa te echará.
 An outsider will be the one who will drive you out
 of your house.

El miedo guarda la viña.
 Fear protects the vineyard.

Ni bebas agua que no veas, ni firmes cartas que no
 leas.
 Don't drink water you have not seen, nor sign
 letters you have not read.
 A warning to beware of the source.

Papelito habla.
 Paper speaks.
 This is advice to have documents rather than
 promises for any serious affair.

Las palabras se las lleva el viento.
 Words are carried away on the wind.
 The other side of the previous proverb.

La palabra convence, pero el ejemplo arrasa.
 Words may convince, but example is
 overwhelming.

Nadie escarmienta en cabeza ajena.
 Nobody learns from another person's experiences.

TRADITIONAL ADVICE AND STRATEGY

A *buen entendedor, pocas palabras.*
For a good listener, few words.

A person able (or willing) to understand requires just a few words to get the idea.

A *gua pasada no mueve molinos.*
Downstream water does not turn mills.

Even if we did something right in the past, it cannot be used as an excuse not to do the right things today. Similarly: "A ship doesn't sail with yesterday's wind." I apply this in all of my relationships.

A *enemigo que huye, puente de plata.*
For an enemy that runs away, make a silver bridge.

A *l amigo y al caballo, nunca hay que cansarlos.*
Never tire out your friend and your horse.

In the recent past, a man's life could depend on a well-rested horse, and today, could depend on a friend that is not tired or has not been tried too harshly. This is one of my life's core values.

A *rbol que crece torcido, nunca su tronco endereza.*
A tree that grows crooked will never become straight.

Once bad habits are formed they are nearly impossible to change. This happens mainly in one's formative years, for good or bad.

Al que le venga el saco, que se lo ponga.
Whom the coat fits should wear it.
What I just said doesn't apply to everyone, you know who you are.

A ver si como roncas duermes.
Let's see if you sleep as well as you snore.
This is a challenge to someone who says they are very good at something to prove it.

Arrieros somos y en el camino andamos.
We're cattle drivers and we share the roads.
A reminder that this world is small, and we are bound to meet the same people again. It can also warn someone: "You got me this time, but someday I'll get you back."

A la fuerza, ni las gallinas ponen, ni los zapatos entran.
With force, the hens will not lay eggs and the shoes will not fit.
When you try to force people or animals, they resist.

A la ocasión la pintan calva.
Opportunity is bald.
The meaning of the proverb is: an opportunity may knock ever so softly, and you need to be diligent to make good use of it. The figure of speech is that it is easy to grab a long haired person that runs by, but not so easy if he is bald, so requires more attentiveness to grab the opportunity.

A lo hecho, pecho. (Ya lo hecho, hecho está.)
What is done is done.

Al cabo de cien años todos seremos calvos.
We all will be bald when we're 100 years old.

Nesting baskets of natural plant fibers woven
by Tarahumara women

Al que no ha usado huaraches, la correas le sacan sangre.

If someone has never worn sandals before, the straps will make the feet bleed.

Hard work, that a person is not used to, will be painful.

Al mejor cazador se le va la liebre.

Even the best hunter misses a shot once in a while.

Cada quién es el arquitecto de su propio destino.

Every person is the architect of his own destiny.

Cada cabeza es un mundo.

Every head is a whole world.

This reminds us that every person has a whole, unique world inside his or her head.

Cuando las barbas de tu vecino veas cortar, echa las tuyas a remojar.

When you see your neighbor's beard has been shaven, better start soaking your own beard.

This means that when we see something happening around us, get prepared, because it is likely to happen to us as well. (A beard is easier to shave after it's been soaked.)

Cría fama y échate a dormir.

Become famous and you get to sleep.

Once fame or a comfortable position has been achieved, there is no longer need to prove oneself.

Desde atrás de la barrera cualquiera le grita "cobarde" al torero.

From behind the barrier (a safe spot inside the bullring) anyone can call the bullfighter a coward.

This teaches us to not criticize another's performance if we are not in the same situation as he is.

Donde pone el ojo, pone la bala.

Wherever he sets his eye he can put a bullet.

This is said of a person who is a dead shot or very good at doing something.

Dondequiera que fueres, haz lo que vieres.

Wherever you go, do as you see done.

Abide by the customs of the place you are in. ("When in Rome, do as the Romans do," was advice from St. Ambrose to St. Augustine in the 4th century.)

Del dicho al hecho hay mucho trecho.

From saying to doing, there is a long distance.

El respeto al derecho ajeno es la paz.

Peace is respecting the rights of others.

El que sabe, sabe.
Whoever knows, knows.

This is said in recognition of someone who demonstrates their expertise at something.

El ayer ya acabó y el mañana no existe. Todo lo que tengo es hoy.
Yesterday is gone and tomorrow does not exist. All I have is now.

El valiente es valiente hasta que el cobarde quiere.
The strong man remains so only as long as the coward wishes.

This refers to a bully who remains so until the other people confront him.

El que la hace, la paga.
He who does it, pays for it.

Whoever does something bad will pay for it.

El que no llora, no mama.
The baby that does not cry will not get to nurse.

"The squeaky wheel gets the grease."

Es mejor morir de pie que vivir de rodillas.
It is better to die on your feet than to live on your knees.

(Attributed to the great Mexican revolutionary Emiliano Zapata (1877–1919) and quoted by President Franklin D. Roosevelt in 1941.)

El cobarde muere cien veces.
The coward dies a hundred times.

A coward afraid of dying is as if he died every time he is in fear. (A paraphrase from *Julius Caesar* by Shakespeare.)

E_xplicación no pedida, acusación dada._
Explanation not asked for, accusation leveled.
If an explanation is given before we ask for it, we assume the person giving the explanation is guilty.

E_l buen paño en el arca se vende._
A good piece of cloth gets sold before taking it out of the crate.
Good quality goods (or people) do not need advertising to get sold, or noticed, right away.

E_l que menos corre, vuela._
The slowest runner flies.
This advises us not to judge lightly on appearances, as that person may be very skilled at something else.

E_n la casa del jabonero, el que no cae, resbala._
In the soap maker's home, whoever doesn't fall, slips.
This warns that in a dangerous situation we're likely to have an accident.

E_n martes trece, ni te cases, ni te embarques, no de tu casa te apartes._
On Tuesday the thirteenth, don't get married, don't board a ship, don't go out of your home.
An old superstition that Tuesday the 13th was unlucky.

E_l que ríe al último, ríe mejor._
Whoever laughs last laughs best.

G_enio y figura hasta la sepultura._
Personality and figure will be unchanged until the grave.
This recognizes that certain qualities of people are unchanged throughout life.

Colorful masks of an owl, a three-faced king, and two birds

Estoy como niño chiquito con juguete nuevo.
I am as happy as a little kid with a new toy.

Hablando del rey de Roma, y el que se asoma.
Speaking of the King of Rome, and he comes by.

This is said when, while talking about someone, that very person shows up.

Los pueblos tienen los gobiernos que se merecen.
Countries have the governments they deserve.

Los usos se hacen costumbres, y las costumbres se hacen ley.
The common practices become customary, then the customary becomes law.

I was taught this is how most laws originated.

Las cosas de palacio van despacio.
Affairs related to the palace go slow.

This recognizes the slow bureaucracy of government.

Lo cortés no quita lo valiente.
Being courteous does not mean one is not brave.

Lo paseado y lo bailado, nadie me lo quita.
All I've traveled and all the dancing I've done nobody can take from me.

This praises the enjoyment of life every day, for simple accomplishments like visiting a new place or dancing.

La gente dudará de lo que digas, pero creerá lo que hagas.
People may question what you say, but will believe what you do.

As applied to parenting: "Parents can tell but never teach, unless they practice what they preach."

La letra con sangre entra.
Literacy/reading enters with blood.

Learning is something you "sweat blood" to do. This saying perhaps exaggerates the effort and dedication necessary to achieve a difficult goal like literacy or a college degree.

La tercera es la vencida.
Third time is a charm.

Las cosas se toman como de quien vienen.
Things are taken according to whom they come from.

This teaches us to be attentive to who is saying something, and give weight to them accordingly.

Las paredes oyen.
Walls listen.

This advises us of being careful what we say and where.

Lo que bien se aprende jamás se olvida.
What is thoroughly learned is never forgotten.

Lo que se ve no se juzga.
What is obvious (seen in plain sight) is never questioned.

Mátalas callando.
Kill them quietly.

This recognizes somebody's stealth and effectiveness to accomplish something, either good or bad. It can also mean that we should do our work quietly and well, without bragging.

Más vale prevenir que lamentar.
It is better to prevent than lament.

"An ounce of prevention is worth a pound of cure."

Más vale caer en gracia que ser gracioso.
It is better to delight than to be a clown.

This praises the pleasing, gracious social approach over the flashy, loud one.

Más vale malo conocido que bueno por conocer.
Better a known bad one than a good one that is unknown.

This says that a known situation (or person), even if imperfect, gives certainty, rather than giving that up for an unknown situation.

Más vale un "toma" que dos "te daré."
It is better to say once "take this one" than twice "I will give you."

There is higher value in something concrete and real than in big promises.

Más vale paso que dure que trote que canse.
It is better to walk at a long-lasting pace than to run and get tired soon (and never finish).

No que no tronabas, pistolita?
Pistol, didn't you tell me you wouldn't fire?

This is a phrase of triumph. It is said when something is accomplished that friends or bystanders said could not happen, like "I don't think you can start that engine." The operator will use this phrase after he successfully starts the engine.

No me duras ni para el arranque.
You won't outlast me even at the start.

This is a challenge to a person whom one does not consider worthy of a long run or whom one has doubts about.

No dejes camino real por vereda.
Do not leave a highway to take a shortcut.

No hay atajo sin trabajo.
There is no shortcut that will not require work as well.

No hay rosa sin espinas.
There is no rose without thorns.

One of many meanings is: be aware of the price that we will pay for something we greatly desire.

No necesito vejigas para nadar.
I do not need floaters (personal flotation devices) to swim.

I can make it on my own and don't need any help to get my job done.

No por mucho madrugar amanece más temprano.
Waking up earlier does not make sunrise happen any earlier.

This recognizes that, even if we are in a great hurry, some things just take their time.

Mayan pottery sculpture of three figures, one is being carried by the other two.

N *unca es tarde si la dicha es buena.*
It is never too late to have good enjoyment.

Nunca juzgues mal un año hasta que pase
diciembre.
Never say it was a bad year until December is over.

No te revientes reata, que es el último jalón!
**Dear rope, don't snap on me just yet; this is the
last pull!**

This is encouragement to somebody to just keep the
effort a little longer, as the task is almost complete
and must be finished.

Poco veneno no mata.
A small amount of poison will not kill.
This suggests that a little danger won't harm us.

Una vez al año no hace daño.
Once a year will not be harmful.

Para un barco sin puerto, cualquier viento es bueno.
For a ship without a port, any wind is good.

Ojos que no ven, corazón que no siente.
Eyes that don't see, heart that doesn't feel.
This is similar to "ignorance is bliss." It can refer
to a person who is not aware of what is happening
around them, essentially unconscious.

Porque te conozco campana, no te vuelvo a repicar.
**Because I know you, bell, I shall not toll you
again.**
I got burnt once already, I will not make the same
mistake again.

Puede venderle nieve a un esquimal.
They can sell snow to an Eskimo.
This is said of a person who is extremely
accomplished at something.

Quien a hierro mata, a hierro muere.
Whoever kills with iron dies by iron.
"Who lives by the sword dies by the sword."
(Paraphrase of *The Holy Bible*, Matthew 26:52)

Quien da primero, da dos veces.
Who hits first hits twice.
This suggests that the value of hitting first is double
any blow that follows.

An animated folk-art zebra

Quien fue a la villa perdió su silla.
Who leaves the house loses his seat.

When you leave, someone else will take your place.

Quien nada no se ahoga.
The person who knows how to swim will not drown.

Sólo el que carga el costal sabe lo que trae adentro.
Only the sack bearer knows what's inside of it, or the reason for carrying that load.

We don't know what another's burden is, nor why they have it.

Ya no siento lo duro sino lo tupido.
I am not feeling the strength of the blows but how many they are.

This is said by a person who is overwhelmed, not with one major task, but with too many small ones.

Sarna con gusto, no pica.
   Scabies with joy don't itch.
   This means that sometimes discomfort is negligible if the prize is worth it.

Una cadena siempre se rompe en el eslabón más débil.
   A chain always breaks at the weakest link.

Ojo por ojo, diente por diente.
   An eye for an eye, a tooth for a tooth.
   (*The Holy Bible*, Exodus 21:24)

Ver la paja en el ojo ajeno y no ver la viga en el propio.
   Seeing the splinter in the neighbor's eye, but not the beam in one's own eye.
   (Paraphrased from *The Holy Bible*, Matthew 7:3)

Ves la tempestad y no te hincas.
   You see the storm and yet are unconcerned.
   This is said of a person who just doesn't understand that the situation is critical.

Yerba mala nunca muere.
   A really bad weed never dies.
   This is applied to the resilience of either bad influences or people.

Yo no vengo a ver si puedo, sino porque puedo, vengo.
   I am not coming to see if I can, but because I can, I come.
   Or, I have made it this far, and I am certain I can perform the task at hand.

A black carved-and-pierced pot

Yo *sin verla no me caso.*
I will not marry the girl if I don't see her first.

Figuratively speaking, this means: I will not commit
to it if I don't know all of the details first.

Zapatero a tus zapatos.
Shoemaker, stick to your shoes.

Perform what you're skilled at. "Stick to your
knitting."

Todo cabe en un jarrito, sabiéndolo acomodar.
**Everything fits in a little jar if you know how to
use the space wisely.**

FROM MY FAMILY
(I grew up hearing these sayings.)

A *palabras de borracho, oídos de cantinero. (Dad)*
Pay bartender ears to drunkard's words.

Listen to the words of each person in a way that is
appropriate to that person.

A *palabras necias, oídos sordos. (Dad)*
For stupid words, deaf ears.

A *mor, dinero y cuidado, no puede dejar de ser
notado. (Mom, Grandma)*
Love, money, and care will always be noticed.

It is impossible to hide care, love, or money.

A *unque la mona se vista de seda, mona se queda.
(Grandma)*
**Even though a monkey gets dressed up in silk,
she is still a monkey.**

C *ada uno habla de la feria según como le va en
ella. (Mom)*
**Everyone speaks of the county fair according to
his own experience.**

This means that two different people can have
different experiences in the same situation, and will
tell very different stories about it.

C *ree el león que todos son de su condición. (Mom)*
The lion believes all are like himself.

This could mean that someone used to doing things
in a certain way will expect others to behave in the
same way; or, someone who feels guilty will suspect
others of the same sin.

Mayan sculpture of mother and child

Si *la juventud supiera, si la vejez pudiera. (Dad, Grandpa)*
If only youth knew; if only old age could.

Date *a deseo, y olerás a apoleo, date a seguido y olerás a podrido. (Grandma)*
Give yourself sparingly and let other people desire you, and you will smell like a flower. Give yourself too often and you will smell rotten.

Apoleo is a very good-smelling flower. This teaches us not to overwhelm other people with our presence, but let them long for our company so they enjoy it when they have it. And, if you overwhelm other people, they will avoid you.

Como te ves, me vi, como me ves, te verás.
(Grandma)

Just as you see yourself, I did. Just as you see me, you will.

This is said from an old person to a young one.

Cuando el río suena, es que agua lleva. *(Mom)*

When the river is making noise, it is carrying a lot of water.

Pay attention to the context of things and the signals; they will often tell us what is happening or what is about to happen.

¿**D**esde cuándo los patos le tiran a las escopetas? *(Dad)*

Since when are the ducks shooting the shotguns?

Dad used to say this when we as children attempted to correct him.

Del rayo te salvas, pero de la raya, no. *(Mother-in-law)*

You may escape from a lightning bolt, but not from "the line" (your time to die).

El dinero no es lo primero, pero es lo segundo. *(Father-in-law)*

Money is not the first thing (to worry about), but it is right next to it.

Dime con quién andas, y te diré quién eres. *(Mom, Dad)*

Tell me who you hang out with, and I will tell you who you are.

Teaches us to choose our friends wisely, as they will influence us to become like them.

Folk-art Madonna and Child with angels

Échate ese trompo a la uña. (Dad)
Try to balance this top on your fingernail.

A *trompo* is a traditional Mexican toy, a fast spinning wooden top with a steel point, similar to a gyroscope. The hardest trick to perform is to make it dance on one's fingernail. The meaning is: try to match this.

Él que se enoja, pierde. (Mom)
Whoever gets angry, loses.

If you lose your temper, you lose. This was one of the toughest and most useful lessons of my childhood: even if you had reason to feel upset or were the offended party, the sole fact that you lost your temper made you lose. I owe a lot of who I am today to this lesson.

El agua sola agarra su nivel. *(Dad)*
Water seeks its own level.

By this, Dad meant that even if there was an abnormal situation, things would return to normal on their own, so it was useless to distress over them.

El flojo y el mezquino recorren siete veces el camino. *(Mom)*
The lazy and the petty will run the same road seven times.

This advises us to get things done right the first time, otherwise we will have to do the work again and again until it is right.

El que come y canta, loco se levanta. *(Mom)*
He who sings and eats will arise crazy, or **whoever sings while eating will end up crazy.**

Mom used to say this so we would be quiet during meals (a baseless threat).

El que busca, encuentra. *(Mom)*
What you look for you find.

Besides the obvious meaning, this was used by my mom at home when we were being so unruly that we got a well-deserved timeout or a slap: you got what you asked for.

El que mucho abarca, poco aprieta. *(Mom)*
Whoever wants to do too much does not do anything well.

This warns us against spreading ourselves too thin, doing few things right.

De médico, poeta y loco, todos tenemos un poco. *(Mom)*
We all have a little bit of physician, poet, and madman in us.

A Day of the Dead figurine, a fancy lady in hat and big skirt.
This holiday honors ancestors and the recently deceased.

E *l hambre se quita comiendo, el sueño se quita durmiendo, pero lo tarugo, ni a trompicones. (Great-grandmother Isabel)*

The cure for hunger is to eat, the cure for tiredness is to sleep, but there is no cure for stupidity.

E *l que compra lo que no necesita termina por vender lo que sí necesita. (Great-grandmother Isabel)*

Whoever buys what he does not need, ends up having to sell something that he really needs.

This teaches us to not spend resources on unnecessary things, or we risk losing necessities.

El que con lobos anda, a aullar se enseña. *(Dad)*
Whoever walks with wolves will learn how to howl.
This teaches us to be careful who we befriend since
their manners and customs will influence us greatly.

El sol de invierno es como el amor del yerno, quema
pero no calienta. *(Grandma)*
**Winter's sun is like the son-in-law's love: burns
you, but doesn't warm you up.**

El sordo no oye, pero compone. *(Mom)*
The deaf cannot hear, but do make up stories.
Somebody who does not know the whole story will
make up the rest out of imagination.

En casa del herrero, azadón (cuchillo) de palo. *(Dad)*
**In the household of the blacksmith, wooden hoe
(or knife).**
This warns against performing a skilled craft to make
a living but failing to provide the same skill in our
own household. (My Dad's version is with "hoe," the
traditional version uses "knife.")

En el arca abierta, hasta el justo peca. *(Dad)*
In the open ark, even the honest will commit sin.
This advises against leaving temptations available
to other people, even if they appear honest. This is
similar to: a lock will just keep an honest person
honest.

En el modo de agarrar el taco se conoce al tragón.
(Dad)
**You can tell if someone will eat a lot of tacos
from the way they hold the first one.**
If somebody is good at something, you can see it as
soon as they start.

Ceramic sculpture of a Mixtec priest

E *n el país de los ciegos, el tuerto es rey. (Mom)*
In the country of the blind men, the one eyed person is King.

A unique skill is very noticeable where it is scarce or nonexistent even if, by other standards, it would be deemed imperfect.

E *nseñó el cobre. (Dad)*
The copper showed up.

This phrase comes from a jewelry context. Cheap jewelry has a copper core and golden plating, even though it may look like solid gold. A common test is to punch a little hole in an inconspicuous area and put a drop of nitric acid on it. The acid reacts with copper in any form, turns green, and gives away the poor quality. This is said of a person who did not pass the "acid" test, like honesty, responsibility, etc.

El que se acuesta con niños, orinado amanece. *(Mom)*
Whoever goes to bed with children wakes up wet.

This warns of the overall lack of trustworthiness of immature people, regardless of their ages. In general, it advises us to be aware with whom we are dealing and what they are able or not able to do. It is like an English proverb, "Whoever sleeps with dogs gets bitten by fleas."

Es pura llamarada de petate. *(Mom)*
It is just a bright but short lived flame.

A *petate* is a mat made from palm leaves, which will burn rapidly and with very bright flame, but shortly. Mom used this when, after an initial burst of energy, someone would fail to finish the task.

Juventud, divino tesoro. *(Mom)*
Youth, divine treasure.

Lo que es parejo no es chipotudo. *(Mom)*
What is even is bumpless.

This means that if a deal is fair, it has to be fair for both parties. (*Parejo* in Spanish means both "even" and "fair," depending on the context.) Mom used this when she caught somebody trying to trick her.

No por que me vean de lana crean que soy borrego. *(Mom)*
The fact that you see I have wealth does not mean I am naive.

Luz de la calle y oscuridad de su casa. *(Mom)*
Streetlight outside but darkness at home.

This is said of a person who acts very different in social situations than in their personal, private life; usually worse in private.

La ociosidad es madre de todos los vicios.
(Mom, Dad, Grandma, everyone)

Idleness is the mother of all vices.

"Idle hands are the devil's workshop."

Más sabe el diablo por viejo que por Diablo.
(Grandma)

The devil knows more due to his old age than due to the fact that he is the devil.

This acknowledges the wisdom gained through life's experience.

Más vale un mal arreglo que un buen pleito.
(Grandpa)

It is always better to come to a bad agreement than to a good fight.

My grandfather was a renowned lawyer, and this saying was one of his favorites.

No te pongas con Sansón a las patadas. *(Dad)*

Don't get in a kicking match with Samson.

This means to weigh an opponent (or situation). Don't get in trouble with someone or something obviously superior.

Mucho ayuda el que no estorba. *(Mom)*

Whoever is not in the way is already a great help.

One of my mom's favorite sayings.

No confundas la gimnasia con la magnesia. *(Dad)*

Don't confuse the gymnastics with the gypsum.

(Magnesia or talc is what gymnasts put on their hands to avoid slipping on the apparatus.) This means that just because we know something similar does not make us an expert, or be clear on this task. Dad used this as a warning when we were about to make a big mistake.

The sun is a favorite motif in Mexican folk art, here as a golden mirror over a side table in a sitting room.

No soy monedita de oro, para caerle bien a todo mundo. *(Mom)*

I am not a gold coin to suit perfectly to everyone.

I accept the fact that there are people who just don't like me, no matter how good or valuable I am.

No dejes para mañana lo que puedas hacer hoy. *(Mom and Dad)*

Don't put off for tomorrow what you can do today.

Advice against procrastination.

No te duermas en tus laureles. *(Dad)*
Don't sleep on your laurels.

Laurel wreathes were given as signs of victory to Olympic winners. This means: even if you were a winner, keep working or you may lose your position. Also: don't be overconfident, even if you are already enjoying success.

No me hables al tiro. (Dad)
Don't talk to me while I'm aiming.

Dad meant: don't distract me, I'm concentrating on this right now.

No digas "la burra es parda" hasta que tengas la zalea en la mano. (Dad)
Don't say "the donkey was brown" until you have his hide in your hand.

Be certain to have evidence at hand before giving information out, making a decision or judgment, or taking an action. I also owe a lot of who I am today to this lesson.

Para que la cuña apriete, tiene que ser del mismo palo. (Grandma)
In order for a wedge to be tight, it has to be made of the same wood as the rest of the piece (in an axe handle, for instance).

This means that the same kind of person is the most effective influence on a second person.

Primero te escandaliza, luego lo ves normal, y terminas por hacerlo. (Great-grandmother Isabel)
First you get shocked, then you see it as normal, and you end up doing it.

This is a warning to separate ourselves from customs or situations that are not compatible with our morals while we are still shocked by them, as constant exposure may eventually cause us to do them.

Tanto peca el que mata la vaca como el que le agarra la pata. (Mom, Dad)
Both the one who kills the cow and the one who holds it down are equally guilty.

Folk-art crucifix with Holy Family

Quien ama el peligro, en él perece. *(Dad, Grandpa)*
Whoever loves danger will die in it.

No te metas entre las patas de los caballos.
Don't crawl through horses' feet.

Keep out of dangerous situations.

Se me echó mi mejor mula. *(Dad)*
My best mule just quit on me.

Dad meant: I am counting on you, don't give up just yet, to get my brother or me back on task.

Vas en caballo de la hacienda. *(Dad)*
You're riding a horse from the hacienda.

This means that you have an unusual advantage or protection on some enterprise. Make good use of it.

Siempre que ven caballo se les ofrece viaje. *(Mom)*
They always need to go somewhere when they see a horse.

This criticizes opportunistic people who like to take advantage of other's resources or who believe they can take whatever they see.

Palo dado, ni Dios lo quita. *(Mom)*
Once one has been hit with a stick, not even God can undo it.

Accept what has already happened and move on. Mom would say this when I would fall off my bike.

Si tu mal tiene remedio, para qué te apuras, y si no tiene, para qué te apuras. *(Father-in-law)*
If your illness (or problem) has a cure, why do you worry? And if it doesn't, why do you worry?

This warns that worrying doesn't help resolve anything, but it makes us miserable.

~